18th Century Costume

in National Museums Liverpool

Book production by The Bluecoat Press, Liverpool
Book design by March Design, Liverpool
Printed by Tenon & Polert
Photography by David Flower

Front cover Silk brocade sack-back gown or robe à la Française, c1765-70. (detail)

ISBN 1 902700 01 5

Acknowledgments

I would like to thank all those who have been involved in the production of this publication, which, I hope, will be the first in a new series focusing chronologically upon National Museums Liverpool's extensive collection of European costume. In particular, thanks are due to David Flower for the excellent photographs, Annie Lord and her colleagues in the Textile Conservation Department for cleaning and conserving all of the items featured here, and Jean-Anne Kelly for making the reproduction corsets and other supporting under-pinnings which were needed to prepare the garments for photography. Clare Browne of the Victoria and Albert Museum's Department of Textiles and Dress and Miles Lambert of the Gallery of English Costume, Manchester, very kindly gave their opinions on the dates of the silk brocades. I am also grateful to Mike March and Colin Wilkinson of The Bluecoat Press for all their work on the design and production of the book.

18th Century Costume

in National Museums Liverpool

Pauline Rushton

NATIONAL MUSEUMS **LIVERPOOL**

Introduction

National Museums Liverpool has a large collection of European costume, covering the period from about 1700 to the present day. Most of it has been acquired by donation since 1945 although items are occasionally purchased in order to fill gaps in the collection. All aspects of male and female costume are represented, including indoor and outdoor clothing, underwear, shoes, hats, jewellery and other accessories. The collection is particularly strong in women's costume for the period between 1840 and 1940, although in recent years additional emphasis has been placed upon collecting material dating from 1940 to the present day, especially designer-made items and High Street fashion.

Some 40 or more garments in the collection date from the 18th century and can be used to trace the main features of fashionable dress during that time. A selection of them, representing the best examples of their kind, are shown here. This publication is divided into three sections, covering women's dress, men's dress and a mixed group of examples from both areas. A number of gaps in the collection of men's costume have been filled with the help of portraits from the Walker Art Gallery. One child's garment, the earliest in the collection, is also featured.

All the garments illustrated here are typical of the forms of clothing worn by the upper and middle classes, which are now preserved in many museum collections, but they do not, unfortunately, include examples of the clothes worn by more ordinary men and women. The clothes of 18th century working people have largely disappeared because they were usually worn out and then discarded. The wealthier could afford to change their clothes as fashions changed but often kept garments that had become outdated. In time, these items have entered museum collections. Today, they can provide us with a wonderful, if incomplete, picture of how people dressed over 200 years ago.

Opposite Man's white silk satin waistcoat, with stem stitch and satin stitch embroidery, c1775-95 (detail) *see page 41.*

Women's dress

Women's underwear consisted of two main garments, a loose-fitting linen or cotton shift, and a pair of stays, the 18th century term for a corset. Drawers were not generally worn until the first decade of the 19th century. The stays were worn over the shift, together with a number of linen or cotton underpetticoats which fastened at the waist with tapes. A quilted petticoat might be worn outermost for added warmth. Pockets were not integrated into women's clothing until the early 19th century and during the 18th were worn as separate items, fastened around the waist over the petticoats by means of tapes and reached by a slit in both side seams of the main gown. They could be worn singly or in pairs. Stockings of knitted silk or linen were fastened above the knee with garters.

The shift was cut square and fell to below knee level. Any extra width required at the sides or beneath the arms was achieved by inserting triangular-shaped gussets called *gores*. The neckline was cut wide so that the garment could be slipped easily over the wearer's head, and both the neckline and the elbow-length sleeves could sometimes have narrow frills of fine linen attached to them.

The stays were usually made from linen or cotton canvas stiffened with whalebone, wood or even metal. They laced up the back or the front and fastened over the shoulders with separate straps tied with cord or ribbon. As part of fashionable dress they could be laced very tightly, forming the wearer's body into a cone shape, drawing the waist in and pushing the breasts forward and up. They were laced more loosely if the wearer was engaged in some form of manual work and needed to feel less restricted. Most 18th century women wore stays in public and would only leave them

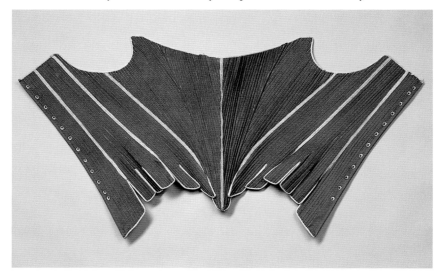

Opposite Hand block-printed cotton open gown, c1775-85 (detail) see page 14.

Pair of women's back-lacing stays of brown cotton canvas lined with linen, with tabs at the waist, c1770-80. They are stiffened with whalebone and, down the centre, with a length of wood known as a busk. The edges are bound with white cotton braid and the surface is decorated with applied bands of pale blue silk.

Silk brocade sack-back gown or robe à la Française, with matching petticoat and reproduction stomacher, c1765-70. The bodice has been re-lined with white cotton and altered, probably for fancy dress wear, during the late 19th century, and the original stomacher is now missing. The back sections of the petticoat have been removed, and the silk blonde lace at the neckline and forming the sleeve ruffles is a 19th century addition.

Side view of the sack-back gown, showing the wide pleat down the back of the bodice.

Pale blue ribbed silk stomacher, backed with linen and embroidered with floral designs in silk and metallic thread, with silk tabs down each side for attachment to a bodice front, c1720-40. The metal-wrapped silk cord lacing down the front is purely decorative, and the narrow tabs at the waist are all boned.

off while in a semi-dressed state in the privacy of their own homes. It was not considered proper, even for working women, to go entirely without stays and most were accustomed to wearing them from childhood, but there were waistcoat-like versions with fewer bones for those who required less support.

From the beginning of the 18th century until the 1780s, support for underpetticoats and gowns came in the form of linen hoops, given shape by cane or whalebone and fastened around the waist with tapes beneath the underpetticoats. Like gowns, they sometimes had side slits to provide the wearer with access to the pockets. Hoops changed in shape and size over time according to the type of dress being worn, the social occasion and the status of the wearer. Some underpetticoats had their own built-in hoops and did not require separate ones.

Outer garments for both men and women were divided according to their level of formality or informality into *dress* or *undress* wear. A typical form of *dress* or formal wear for women, from the early 18th century until the 1770s, was the *sack-back gown* or *robe à la Française*, which took its English name from the voluminous back section of the garment with a wide, inverted pleat falling down the centre back of the bodice. This form of dress was particularly favoured in France, as its alternative name suggests, where clothing tended generally to be more formal, at least for the aristocracy who spent much of their time at Court rather than on their country estates. The sack-back gown, often referred to by contemporaries simply as the sack, was often worn with a matching outer petticoat, visible in the open-fronted skirt, and a stomacher, a separate inverted V-shaped piece of fabric which filled the gap across the bodice front. It was attached to either side of the bodice by means of tapes, ribbons or pins. Stomachers could either match or contrast with the main fabric of the gown and were often beautifully embroidered. They provided an element of change in dress and made it more economical to vary the look of one's gown.

Pale green silk brocade open gown, with linen-lined bodice and sleeves and drawstring neckline, c1770-80. Pale blue quilted silk petticoat, lined with calamanco, mid 18th century. The bodice of the gown laces up the front through the linen lining, which is boned on each side beneath the silk.

Back view of open gown, which has a number of sets of tapes sewn inside the skirt for arranging it à la Polonaise if required.

The sack was worn with a hoop beneath the petticoat in order to hold out the skirts over the hips. The shape created in this way grew very exaggerated, especially for formal occasions during the 1740s and 1750s when it extended into a wide oblong, until it became difficult for the wearer to sit down, pass through doorways or enter carriages. This form was worn only by the very fashionable and most women wore smaller, more manageable hoops with the sack.

A more widespread fashion for most of the 18th century was the *open gown* or *robe à l'Anglaise*, which was a typical form of *undress* or informal wear, especially in England as its name suggests. Confusingly, it was also often referred to as a *nightgown* although it was never worn in bed, where most women wore some form of the shift. The open gown was cut to fall open at the skirts in the front, displaying a petticoat of either matching or contrasting fabric. In this form it was often referred to by contemporaries as a 'gown and coat', with the word 'petticoat' shortened. It could be worn either with a stomacher or with the bodice fastening edge to edge down the front by means of pins or hooks and eyes. Quilted petticoats, with a layer of woollen batting sandwiched between layers of silk, were especially popular beneath open gowns for extra warmth. Unlike the sack-back gown, the open gown's bodice was usually arranged in pleats which lay flat against the back of the body and which sometimes ran through the waistline and into the skirt. This construction was known as a *fourreau* back.

In England, the open gown was sometimes worn with a fine white muslin apron embroidered with whitework decoration, and a similar muslin neck handkerchief, which emphasised still further the gown's informal character. In addition, the hoop could be left off altogether with an open gown or, if worn, was very small. The sleeves of both open and sack-back gowns could be decorated by the addition of separate sleeve ruffles, either of fine lace or of the cheaper embroidered muslin. When further embellished with drawn threadwork, a technique in which selected threads were pulled out of the ground fabric to produce a pattern, and with whitework embroidery, such fine muslin was known as Dresden work after its place of origin. Ruffles were sewn to the edge of the shift sleeves and could be removed for washing or to change the style of the gown.

During the 1770s another fashion emerged in the form of a gown which was gathered up over the hips and at the back, a shape achieved either by pulling the ends of the hem up through the pocket slits at each side, or by tying together several pairs of tapes sewn inside the skirt. This was the gown *à la Polonaise*, which remained popular until the mid 1780s, and largely replaced the sack for formal wear. The petticoat worn beneath, of

Silk brocade open gown and matching petticoat, the bodice and sleeves lined with linen, the bodice front fastening edge to edge with hooks and eyes, c1750-60.

Back view of open gown, showing the fourreau back.

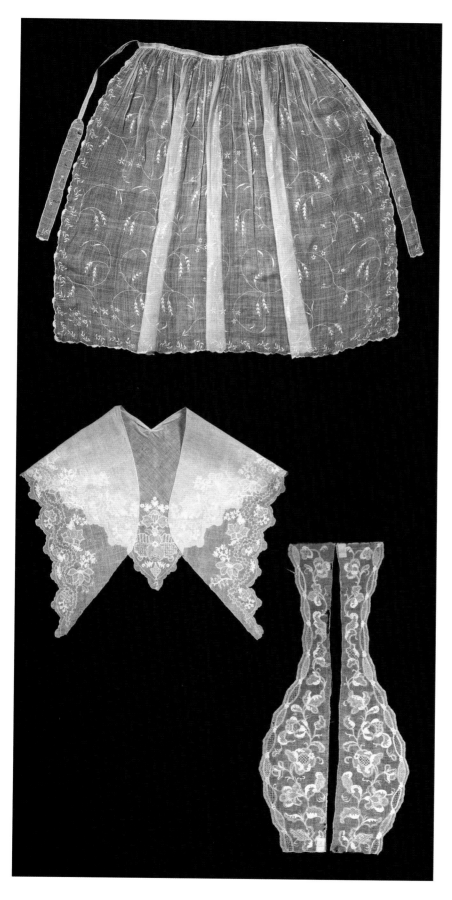

Apron, white cotton muslin embroidered with cotton thread in stem stitch, satin stitch and chainstitch, mid-late 18th century.

Neck handkerchief, white cotton muslin with a floral design worked in white cotton chainstitch, satin stitch and drawn threadwork with needlework fillings, mid-late 18th century.

Pair of sleeve flounces of white cotton muslin with floral design in white cotton chainstitch, satin stitch and drawn threadwork with needlework fillings, early-mid 18th century.

Detail of neck handkerchief.
Detail of sleeve flounce.

Side view of the open gown à la Polonaise. The hem of the skirt is lined with a deep band of cream silk, which has been conserved.

Silk brocade open gown, the bodice and sleeves lined with linen, the skirt arranged à la Polonaise by means of a number of tapes tied together inside, c1775-85. The bodice front fastens edge to edge with pins. Pink quilted silk satin petticoat, lined with calamanco, mid 18th century. Both originally belonged to a Mary Hyde (1730-1832).

Hand block-printed cotton open gown, the bodice and sleeves lined with linen, the skirt arranged à la Polonaise by means of a number of tapes tied together inside, c1775-85. The bodice front fastens edge to edge with pins. The hem at the front has been shortened and a band of silk ribbon added at each side of the skirt. Pink quilted silk petticoat, lined with calamanco, mid 18th century. Both originally belonged to a Mary Hyde (1730-1832).

either a matching or a contrasting fabric, was shorter than those worn earlier and exposed more of the wearer's ankles, making it popular as a walking costume too. The puffed-out shape of the gown was balanced above by the high, elaborately constructed hairstyles which became popular with fashionable women during the 1770s.

Throughout the 18th century, gowns were made in a variety of fabrics but floral silk brocades and damasks were the most common, certainly for sack-back and open gowns. In general, large, extravagantly scrolling floral patterns tended to be popular during the first half of the century, when they could be displayed to best advantage draped over wide side hoops. They gradually gave way, during the second half of the century, to smaller designs until, by the 1780s and 1790s, small floral repeats, narrow stripes and trellis patterns were the norm. Smaller patterns were, in any case, more suited to the puffed up Polonaise style, which did not require large floral repeats to be visible, and they appeared on the lighter weight silks of the period which were known as *lutestrings* or *lustrings*.

Although the size and shape of a fabric's pattern can be a good indication of its date these factors alone cannot be used to date a made up garment. Often, lengths of silk were kept for years and could be used to make gowns of a different style to that found in the period of the fabric's

Side view of the printed cotton open gown à la Polonaise.

initial production. Similarly, a gown could be altered during its lifetime in order to bring it up to date as time went on. In both cases, one can see the high value placed on fabrics by contemporaries and their desire not to waste precious materials.

Printed cotton fabrics were a popular alternative to silk, especially for summer wear, and were very much influenced by the printed cotton *chintzes*, fabrics with glazed surfaces, which had been imported into England from India since the early 17th century. They became so popular that, in 1701, following the lobbying of Parliament by native wool and silk manufacturers who felt their livelihoods threatened, the wearing of imported printed fabrics became illegal. In 1721 this ban was extended to printed fabrics made in England, although it did not end the craze for them, and in 1774 when the ban was finally lifted production increased dramatically to meet the huge demand. Printed cottons remained extremely popular for gowns until the late 1780s when they were replaced for a time by a fashion for white muslin. They reasserted themselves during the last decade of the century when small scale, repeat patterns, often on a dark ground, became the norm.

Women's shoes changed quite dramatically in style during this period. For the first half of the 18th century they had pointed toes and high, curved block-like heels, similar to those worn at the end of the 17th century. They were sometimes worn with matching clogs, which were secured over the shoes with leather ties, in order to protect them from water and mud on the streets. Toes became rounder and heels lower as the century progressed, although by the 1790s the toes of fashionable shoes had once again become very pointed and heels extremely low. For most of the century women's shoes were made from silk brocades, damasks and satins, lined with leather or linen, and very often matched a particular gown. They generally fastened across the instep with fabric straps which threaded through a buckle, made of steel, silver and precious stones or glass pastes, depending upon what the wearer could afford. By the last decade of the century, slip-on shoes without buckles had become more common for women and were often made of leather which sometimes had painted or printed decoration. Throughout the period shoes were made to the same pattern on a straight last, not as a separate left and right fitting, and only took on the shape of the feet through repeated wear.

Opposite Women's shoes, from top to bottom; yellow and white silk brocade with silver metallic thread braid applied to front and red Morocco leather-covered heel, c1730-50; matching clog, red Morocco leather and white pony skin, the original leather tie now missing, c1730-50; pale blue and brown cotton corduroy bound with pale blue silk braid, c1770-90; natural-coloured linen with red Morocco leather-covered heel, embroidered with red, green and yellow floral motif in chainstitch, c1770-90; red Morocco leather bound with red silk braid, c1790-1800; Below yellow kid leather with printed black polka dots and yellow silk ribbon rosette, c1790-1800.

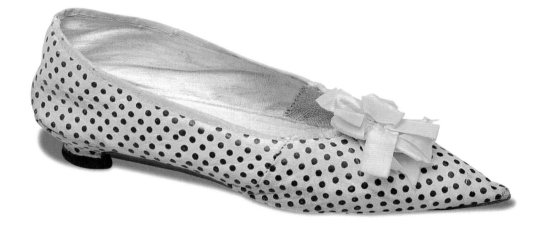

Men's dress

Men's underwear, like women's, consisted of two main garments; a plain white linen shirt, cut long and full, and a pair of linen or cotton drawers, worn beneath the breeches.

The shirt, which was also considered to be outerwear when necessary, opened with a vertical slit at the neck and fastened with tapes or buttons and a small standing band or soft fall collar. It had voluminous sleeves and triangular-shaped gussets beneath the arms, to allow for ease of movement, with the armhole seam cut low so that it sat off the shoulder, across the top of the arm.

Opposite *Man's black silk velvet court suit, c1775-1800 (detail) see page 44.*

Portrait of a Young Man, Richard Caddick, c1775, Walker Art Gallery.
The sitter, possibly the artist himself, wears a fine linen cravat or stock and ruffles on his shirt front.

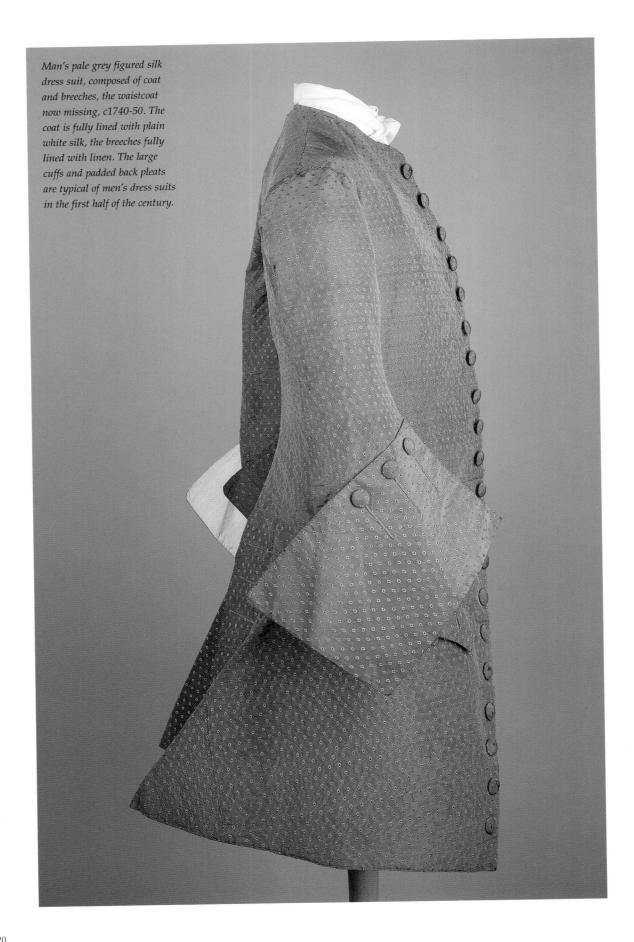

Man's pale grey figured silk dress suit, composed of coat and breeches, the waistcoat now missing, c1740-50. The coat is fully lined with plain white silk, the breeches fully lined with linen. The large cuffs and padded back pleats are typical of men's dress suits in the first half of the century.

Portrait of Sir Robert Clayton, Thomas Gainsborough, 1769, Walker Art Gallery.
Sir Robert wears the typical dress suit of the later 18th century; a buff-coloured silk coat, matching waistcoat and breeches, all trimmed with gold braid, and worn with a fine muslin or lace cravat and sleeve ruffles. He holds a black felt or beaver tricorne hat trimmed with gold braid.

Over the shirt band or collar either a fine linen cravat or a stock was worn, the stock being a ready made-up version of the cravat in pleated linen which fastened at the back of the neck. Both forms were popular throughout the 18th century.

Men's dress or formal suits consisted of three garments; coat, waistcoat and breeches. They could be made of matching or contrasting fabrics and changed gradually in shape and cut over the century. During the first half, coats were cut long, as they had been at the end of the 17th century, and had wide *bucket* cuffs and no collars. Padded pleats to the back of the coat skirts, held in place by wire, buckram lining or some other form of stiff padding such as horsehair, resulted in an outline similar to that of the contemporary female in a hooped gown.

By the second half of the 18th century, the shape of the suit had narrowed considerably. The coat sleeves, cuffs and pleats were all much reduced in size and the fronts became cut away at the sides, revealing more of the waistcoat and breeches. The padded side pleats grew smaller and moved to the back of the coat. During the 1770s a small stand collar appeared on both coat and waistcoat, but initially it lay flat at the neckline. By the 1790s the stand collar of the waistcoat had increased in size and began to rise at the throat, a forerunner of the outrageously exaggerated male collar styles of the early 1800s.

Pair of young man's blue corded silk breeches, fully lined with fustian, the pockets lined with chamois leather, inscribed **Fassett** *in ink on the waistband, c1765-70. They may possibly have belonged to Thomas Fassett (1748-1820) a wealthy resident of Kingston upon Thames, Surrey. Other clothing in the collection is marked* **Fassett, Kingston on Thames** *in the same hand.*

Detail of metal foil and silver wire-covered buttons on the young man's breeches, c1765-70.

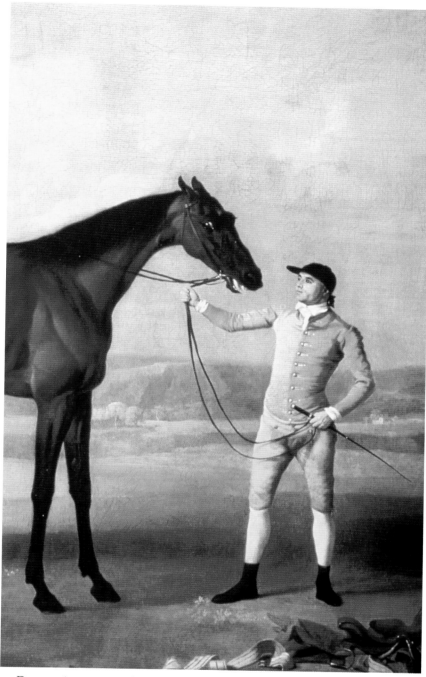

Dress suits were made in a variety of fabrics, with plain ribbed silks and finely-figured silks in small repeat patterns being especially popular. The breeches were cut full at the back and were gathered into the waistband with a laced vent, so as to allow the wearer to sit or ride more comfortably. They fastened at the sides of the knees with buttons or buckles and at the front with buttons, which were concealed, by the second half of the century, by a *fall flap* of the same fabric, buttoning at either side. The flap also gave a smoother line to the top half of the breeches as they were exposed further by the diminishing line of the waistcoat. Braces were only introduced during the 1790s and some surviving late 18th century breeches still have buttons for braces attached to the waistband.

Opposite Detail of silk chainstitch embroidery, including naturalistic rosebuds and pansies, at neckline of waistcoat, and mother-of-pearl buttons with stamped metal foil centres, c1760-70.

Man's pale blue ribbed silk waistcoat, the sleeves, back and lower front skirt lining all of calamanco, the back lining of fustian, labelled **Lady Congreve**, c1760-70.

Suit waistcoats were made either to match or to contrast with the coat and, during the first half of the 18th century at least, could also have full-length sleeves, which were sometimes detachable, for extra warmth. Some had sleeves of *calamanco*, a hard-wearing glazed wool, which was also used for lining women's quilted petticoats. Any areas which were normally concealed beneath the coat, such as sleeves, backs and side sections, were often made of cheaper silks, linen, wool or *fustian*, a mixture of cotton and linen, for the sake of economy. Quilted waistcoats were popular for added warmth in winter.

During the early 18th century waistcoats were long, reaching well down the wearer's thigh and following the lines of the coat. As the century progressed they became shorter and more fitted to the body, reaching to just below the waist by the late 1780s and 1790s. Double-breasted waistcoats also became popular by the end of the century.

The densely-woven wool known as *broadcloth*, since it was woven on the full width of the loom, was also used for dress suits in the first half of the 18th century, often decorated with applied metal braid or embroidery around the collar, cuffs, buttons, pocket flaps and edges. Sometimes a very

decorative woven silk brocade waistcoat would be worn with a plain wool coat and breeches for added effect. The brocade was first woven to shape as two waistcoat fronts before being cut out and assembled as a finished garment.

An alternative to the brocade waistcoat with a plain suit was the embroidered white linen version, worn during the first half of the century. The linen waistcoat was decorated with whitework embroidery and drawn threadwork, commonly worked in large scrolling plant forms, including carnations, poppies and pomegranates, which were adopted from the floral silks of the period. It must have looked very striking when worn with plain dark wool.

Embroidered waistcoats were made in a similar way to those of woven silk brocade. One could buy waistcoat *patterns*, which consisted of the waistcoat fronts, collar, pocket flaps and button tops, worked by a professional embroiderer onto a single square of silk. The pieces would be cut out by a tailor, who would then add the sides, back, lining and interlining to produce the finished garment for the customer.

A favourite form of decoration for men's waistcoats was chainstitch embroidery or *tambourwork*. This usually appeared around the necklines, front and bottom edges and on the pocket flaps of plain or ribbed silk waistcoats, in a variety of coloured silks. This technique, which was brought to Europe from the East around the middle of the 18th century, took its name from the French word for a drum, *tambour*, since the silk was pulled tight over a circular wooden frame, resembling a drum-top, and was then worked with a hook. The silk thread was pulled through the stretched silk fabric from beneath and a chainstitch formed on the surface. Waistcoat silks were worked in this way on larger rectangular frames. During the 1780s and 1790s waistcoats tended to have lighter patterns of embroidery at the collar, edges and pocket flaps, while the ground was scattered with small repeat motifs in embroidered silk.

A very formal type of dress wear for men was the Court suit, worn by the wealthy and aristocratic for such special occasions as attendance at Court. Such suits were usually made of fine silk or silk velvet, heavily embroidered and sequined by professional embroiderers. They were worn with lace-trimmed cravats, lace sleeve ruffles, white silk stockings and black leather buckled shoes. Both the coat and the waistcoat were embroidered to shape then cut out and assembled as garments. The whole ensemble proclaimed the wearer's high social status and wealth.

There were other, more informal, forms of dress available to men during the 18th century. Most popular of these was the wool *frock*, worn with a waistcoat, breeches and top-boots. It was a typically English fashion since life on the English country estate encouraged informality in dress. The *frock*, known by the end of the 18th century as the *frock coat*, had a soft turned-over collar and was not as fitted to the body as the suit coat. The wool broadcloth of which it was generally made was *fulled*, or washed with fuller's earth then stretched and dried and the knap raised with teazels, spiky dried flower heads. The knap was cropped short and beaten flat to produce a densely-finished surface which was warm and water resistant. The cloth was so dense after fulling that the edges did not fray and so required no hem.

Decoration on the frock was generally confined to a narrow band of metallic braid, applied at the collar, cuffs, front edges, pocket flaps and buttons.

Although it began life as a country or sporting form of dress, by about 1770 the frock had become the predominant form of undress wear for men, even in town. It was much copied on the Continent, especially in France where English fashions in menswear were becoming extremely popular.

Men's shoes during the 18th century were generally of leather, unlike women's. They fastened across the instep with a buckle, usually of steel for everyday wear but sometimes of silver set with precious stones or glass pastes for special occasions. Buckles began to disappear by the 1790s, replaced by a fashion for plain leather slip-on shoes. *Top boots* of black leather, so called because the tops were turned down to expose the pale unworked side of the hide, were especially popular in England as undress wear with the frock and breeches. Originally worn only for hunting and other country pursuits, they eventually became an accepted part of town dress for men.

Costume in detail

Opposite *Silk brocade open gown or robe à l'Anglaise, the bodice and sleeves lined with original linen, the skirt conserved and lined with modern cream silk. Petticoat of pale yellow quilted silk lined with calamanco, mid-late 18th century. The brocade of the gown dates from c1736-38, but the garment was made up later, c1770-80. It originally belonged to Agnes Freeland (1749-1825), a doctor's wife from Kirkcudbright, Scotland.*

Side view of open gown, showing the large repeat pattern of scrolling leaves and flowers.

Silk brocade open gown, the sleeves lined with linen, the bodice unlined but stiffened down the back seam with narrow strips of cane, originally covered with paper, c1743-45. Pale pink silk reproduction stomacher and pink quilted silk satin petticoat, lined with calamanco, mid 18th century.

*Back view of open gown,
showing the fourreau back.*

Silk satin brocade open gown, the bodice and sleeves lined with linen, c1750, and pink quilted silk satin petticoat, lined with calamanco, mid 18th century. The bodice of the gown fastens edge to edge down the front with hooks and eyes.

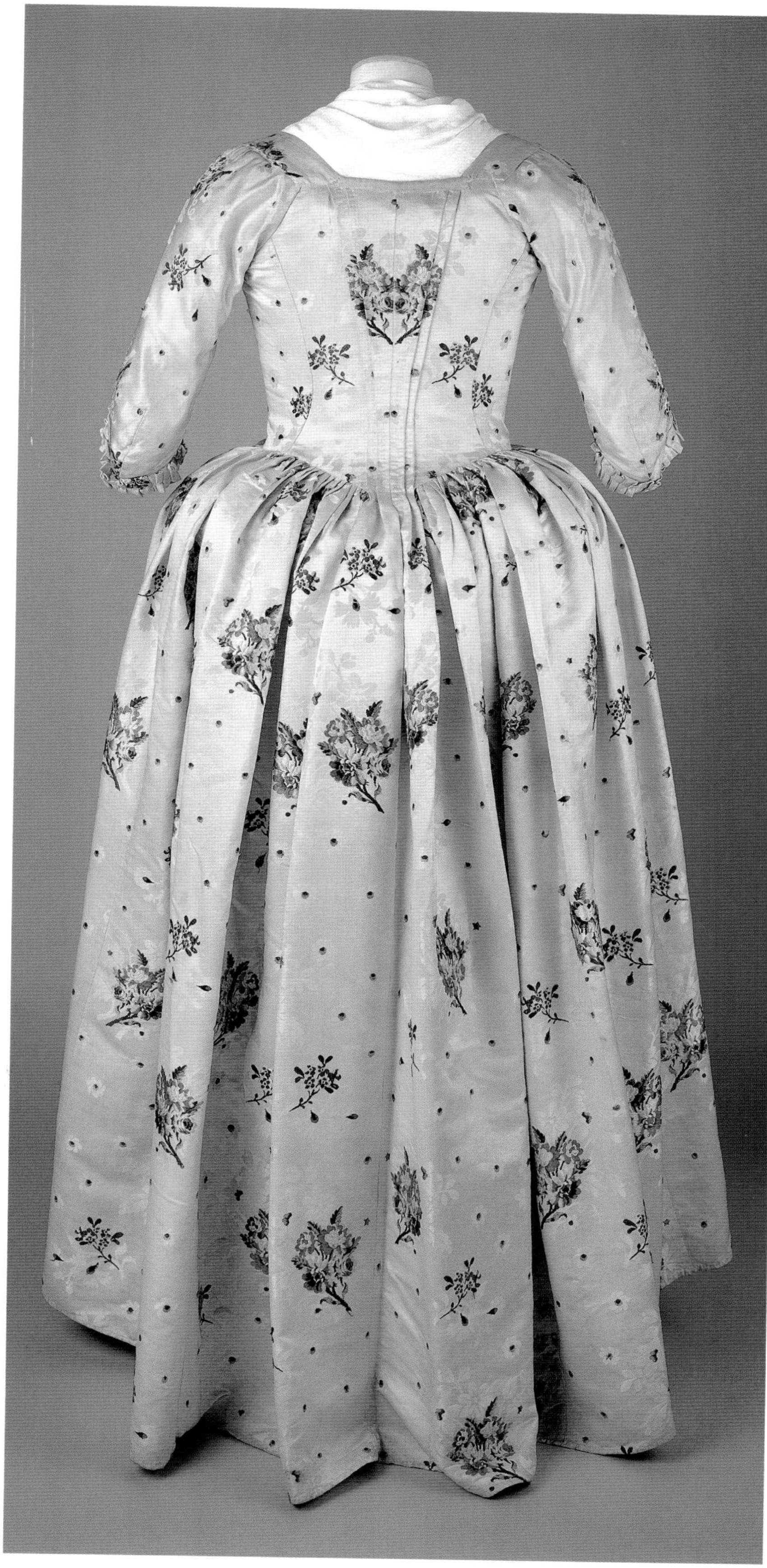

Back view of open gown, showing the fourreau back.

Opposite *Portrait of Richard Gildart, Joseph Wright of Derby, 1768, Walker Art Gallery. The sitter is wearing a fine wool broadcloth coat, waistcoat and breeches. The coat still has rather large bucket cuffs for the time, which had gone out of fashion for younger men by then, but older people often retained the styles of their youth. Gildart, a successful Liverpool sugar merchant, MP and former Mayor of Liverpool, was aged 95 when the portrait was painted.*

Man's white linen waistcoat decorated with drawn threadwork and whitework embroidery, backed and lined with linen, c1720-40.

Detail, showing the elaborate design of carnations and pomegranates in whitework, drawn threadwork and embroidered French knots.

Man's long-sleeved silk and
gilt metal thread brocade
waistcoat, the figured silk
ground woven in a diaper
pattern, c1740-50. The back
is of white corded and
figured silk, the lining of
linen and twilled silk. The
upper parts of the sleeves are
of corded silk, rather than the
expensive brocade, since they
would have been hidden by
the coat when worn.

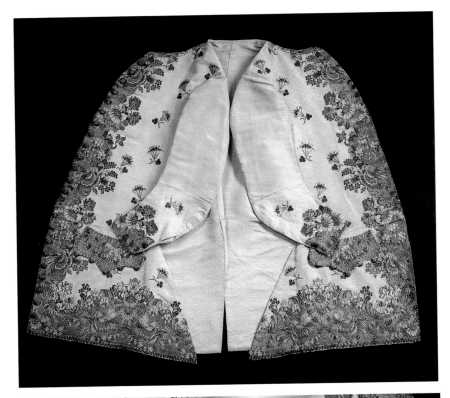

Detail, showing the diaper-
patterned silk used for the
ground and part of the back,
c1740-50.

Man's quilted pink silk satin waistcoat, embroidered in stem stitch and satin stitch, with sequins and metallic silver braid trim. Lined with fustian and plain silk, c1760-80.

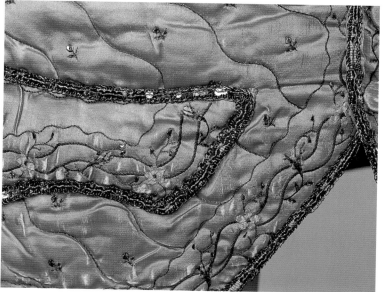

Detail of the pocket flap, showing the metallic braid trim.

Man's white silk satin waistcoat with coloured silk chainstitch embroidery, lined and backed with linen, c1770-80.

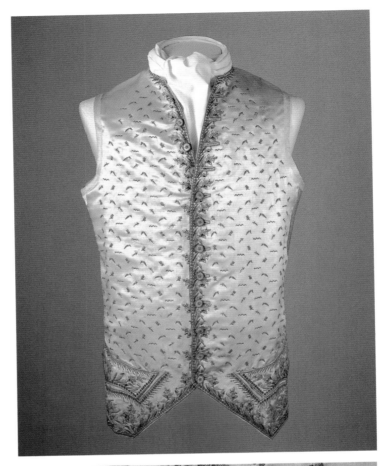

Detail of the chainstitch embroidery. This waistcoat has two embroidered circles incorporated under the left sleevehole, left over from the silk pattern, for covering the buttons, which have been included by the tailor who made it up into the finished garment.

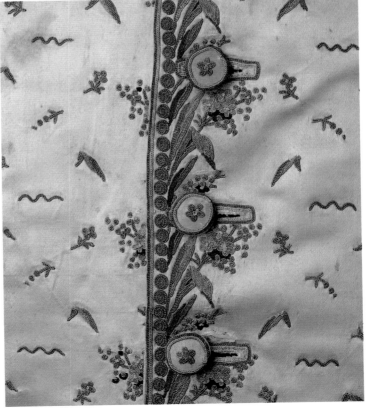

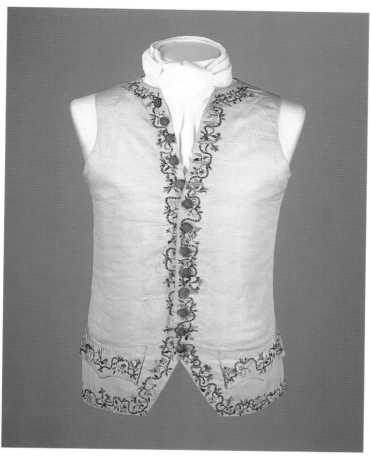

Man's white corded silk waistcoat, backed and lined with fustian and silk, decorated with chainstitch embroidery in silk and silver metallic thread, c1770-80.

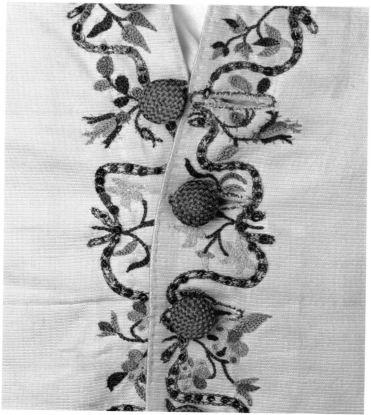

Detail, showing the metallic thread-covered buttons in a basketwork pattern.

Man's white silk satin waistcoat decorated with coloured silk chainstitch embroidery and silk chenille fillings, c1770-80. The back and inner lining are of fustian, the facings and skirt fronts are lined with wool flannel and silk satin.

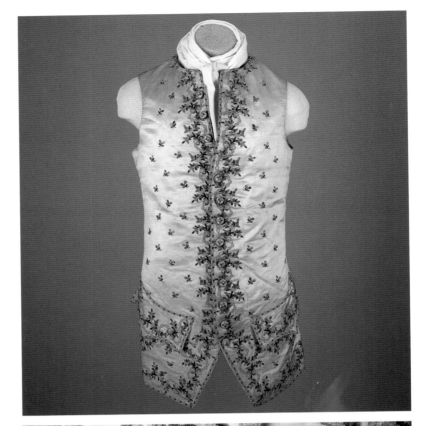

Detail of the bottom edge and pocket flap, showing the silk chenille fillings to the floral motifs. Chenille thread has its fibres fluffed out during the production process to give a soft, furry effect.

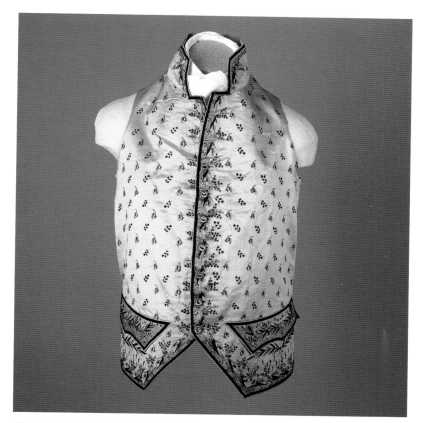

Man's white silk satin waistcoat, possibly from a Court suit, with stem stitch and satin stitch embroidery, c1775-95. The back is of cream wool, the lining of white linen.

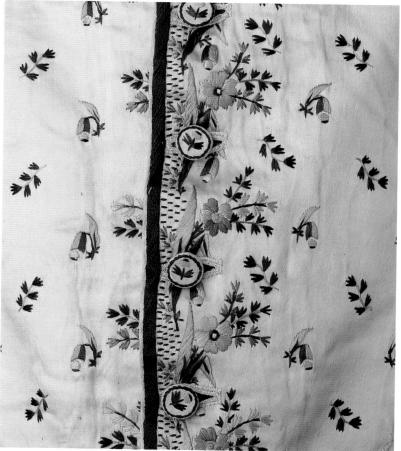

Detail of the embroidery. The satin stitch edging to the fronts, neckline and pocket flaps is so uniform that it resembles a silk binding from a distance.

*Man's white corded silk
waistcoat, possibly from a
Court suit, decorated with
stem stitch and satin stitch
embroidery, French knots,
sequins, silver wire and glass
pastes, c1775-95. The back
and lining are of natural
linen, the facings and skirt
linings of white twilled silk.*

*Detail of the embroidery and
sequined decoration. The silk
net has been applied around
the edges in imitation of lace.*

Man's double-breasted white cotton dimity waistcoat with chainstitch embroidery in pink and green silk and silver metallic thread, c1790-1800. Fully lined and backed with linen and inscribed **AA 93** (possibly the owner's initials and the date, 1793) in ink on the centre back. Dimity is a cotton fabric woven with a slightly raised self-coloured stripe or check.

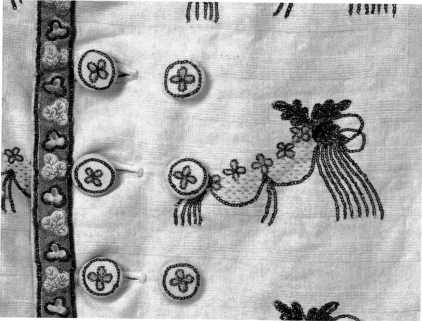

Detail, showing the applied band of printed cotton at the edge of the waistcoat, oversewn with chainstitch embroidery. The silver metallic thread is now tarnished but must have looked very attractive originally, combined with the pink and green silk.

*Man's black silk velvet Court
suit consisting of a coat, silk
satin waistcoat and breeches,
embroidered with stem stitch,
satin stitch, French knots,
sequins, silver wire and glass
pastes, c1775-1800. The
chest area is padded with a
cotton and linen interlining
which appears to be original.*

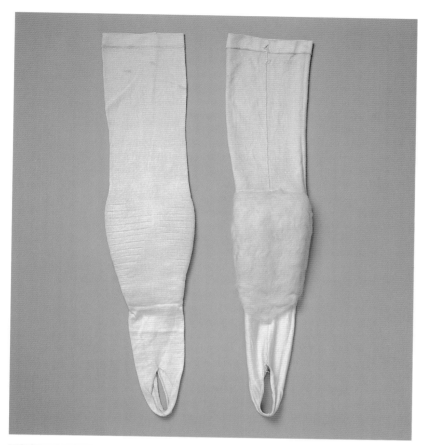

Pair of men's knitted white silk stockings, with lambswool-padded calves, probably worn with a Court suit, c1775-1800. The right stocking is inside out, showing the lambswool lining. A shapely calf was considered very important in the 18th century and some men required a little help in achieving the desired line.

Pair of men's black leather boots, worn by a postillion, the rider of one of the lead horses in a team pulling a carriage, early-mid 18th century. Such long, thick leather boots were necessary to protect the rider's legs while in the saddle.

Child's silk brocade dress, the stomacher-shaped bodice lined with cream silk, c1745-50. The sleeve flounces are of needlerun net, imitating lace, and were added during the 19th century. There are silk brocade leading strings attached at the back of the dress, at each shoulder although they may have been purely decorative for a child of this age. Children were dressed as miniature adults until the last decade of the 18th century.

Opposite Detail of the silk brocade.

Suggested Further Reading

Linda Baumgarten, Eighteenth-Century Clothing at Williamsburg
The Colonial Williamsburg Foundation, 1986

Francois Boucher, A History of Costume in the the West
Thames and Hudson, 1987

Anne Buck, Dress in Eighteenth Century England
B.T. Batsford, 1979

Aileen Ribeiro, Dress in Eighteenth Century Europe, 1715-1789
B.T. Batsford, 1984

Natalie Rothstein (ed.), Four Hundred Years of Fashion
Victoria and Albert Museum, 1984

Jane Tozer & Sarah Levitt, Fabric of Society, A Century of People and their Clothes, 1770-1870
Laura Ashley Ltd, 1983